TADEJ POGAČAR

BIOGRAPHY

How He Became a Cycling Champion

Shara A. Wolff

Disclaimer

This book is planned to give supportive data on web security for kids. It doesn't supplant direction from guardians, gatekeepers, or instructors. While each work has been made to guarantee precision, the quickly changing nature of innovation implies that a few subtleties might become obsolete. Continuously counsel a believed grown-up for guidance on remaining safe on the web, and recall that internet based security is a common obligation. The writer and distributor are not responsible for any activities taken in view of the substance of this book.

TABLE OF CONTENTS

INTRODUCTION

Tadej Pogačar is a professional cyclist from Slovenia who has rapidly risen to prominence in the world of competitive cycling. Born on September 21, 1998, in Komenda, Slovenia, Pogačar exhibited a passion for cycling at a young age. His early exposure to the sport, inspired by the picturesque landscapes of his homeland, laid the foundation for what would become an extraordinary career. Pogačar began his cycling journey with local clubs, where he honed his skills and quickly became known for his remarkable talent.

His breakthrough came in 2019 when he joined UAE Team Emirates. That year, he made headlines by winning three stages of the Tour of California, showcasing his potential as a future star. However, it was in 2020 that Pogačar truly made his mark on the cycling world by winning the prestigious Tour de France at just 21 years old. This victory made him the youngest rider in history to achieve this feat, solidifying his reputation as a formidable competitor. His performance included winning both the general classification and the young rider classification, as well as clinching the mountains classification with his exceptional climbing abilities.

Pogačar's racing style is characterized by his versatility and tenacity. He excels in various terrains, whether climbing steep mountains or sprinting on flat stages. His strategic approach, combined with his strength and stamina, makes him a formidable opponent in any race. Beyond his athletic prowess, Pogačar is known for his humble demeanor and dedication to the sport, earning the admiration of fans and fellow cyclists alike.

Pogačar enjoys a relatively private life, focusing on training and personal interests. He often expresses gratitude for his team and supporters, acknowledging the importance of collaboration in achieving success. As he continues to compete at the highest levels, Tadej Pogačar remains a source of inspiration for aspiring cyclists around the world, exemplifying hard work, resilience, and the pursuit of excellence in the sport.

Tadej Pogačar has had a profound impact on the world of cycling, both through his remarkable achievements and his approach to the sport. Since bursting onto the professional cycling scene, he has redefined what it means to be a young athlete in a traditionally competitive field. His early success, particularly his historic win at the 2020 Tour de France, has not only placed him among the sport's elite but also inspired a new generation of cyclists.

Pogačar's victories have been characterized by their diversity; hc is not just a climber or a sprinter but a complete cyclist capable of excelling in various race conditions. His ability to win across multiple terrains has set a new standard for versatility, compelling other cyclists to adapt and enhance their own skills. He has also been instrumental in elevating the profile of Slovenian cycling on the global stage, bringing attention to a nation that has historically been overshadowed by larger cycling powerhouses.

Pogačar's sportsmanship and humble demeanor have resonated with fans and aspiring athletes alike. He often emphasizes teamwork and acknowledges the role of his teammates and coaches in his success. This approach has fostered a sense of camaraderie within the cycling community and has highlighted the importance of collaboration in achieving individual goals.

Beyond his athletic performance, Pogačar has also engaged with fans through social media, providing insights into his training, races, and personal life. This transparency has helped humanize professional athletes, making them more relatable to fans and inspiring young cyclists to pursue their dreams. His influence extends beyond just race results; he has become a role model, promoting the values of hard work, dedication, and humility.

Tadej Pogačar's impact on cycling is significant. His extraordinary accomplishments have set new benchmarks, while his character and approach have enriched the sport's culture. As he continues to compete, Pogačar's legacy is likely to inspire future generations of cyclists, encouraging them to strive for excellence and to embrace the spirit of sportsmanship.

CHAPTER 1 EARLY LIFE

Tadej Pogačar was born on September 21, 1998, in Komenda, Slovenia, a picturesque town known for its scenic landscapes. Growing up in a supportive family, Tadej was encouraged to pursue his interests from a young age. His parents played a crucial role in nurturing his passion for sports, particularly cycling. As a child, he was active and adventurous, often spending his free time outdoors, exploring the beautiful Slovenian countryside.

Pogačar's introduction to cycling began when he was just a boy. He received his first bicycle at a young age, which sparked his love for the sport. Tadej quickly joined a local cycling club, where he was able to develop his skills and gain valuable experience. His natural talent and determination became apparent as he started participating in local races, where he consistently performed well against older competitors.

As he progressed in his cycling journey, Tadej faced numerous challenges, including tough competition and the demands of training. However, his relentless work ethic and passion for the sport kept him motivated. Throughout his youth, he trained rigorously, balancing his cycling commitments with schoolwork. This dedication paid off as he began to achieve notable results in junior cycling competitions.

During his teenage years, Pogačar's potential caught the attention of professional teams, leading to opportunities for further development. His success in national junior championships and international races propelled him into the spotlight, setting the stage for his transition to professional cycling. By the time he turned 19, he had already established himself as a rising star in the cycling world, demonstrating remarkable talent and a promising future.

Pogačar's early life was marked by a strong foundation of support, determination, and an unwavering passion for cycling. These elements not only shaped him as an athlete but also instilled values of hard work and perseverance that would guide him throughout his illustrious career. His journey from a young boy in Slovenia to a world-renowned cycling champion is a testament to his dedication and the encouragement of his family and community.

Tadej Pogačar's childhood and family background played a vital role in shaping him into the exceptional athlete he is today. Born and raised in Komenda, Slovenia, Tadej was immersed in a supportive and nurturing environment that encouraged his interests and ambitions. His parents recognized his early enthusiasm for sports and made it a priority to foster that passion.

Growing up in a close-knit family, Tadej was often involved in various outdoor activities, which helped develop his physical fitness and love for adventure. His family frequently engaged in cycling outings, introducing him to the sport in a fun and informal way. These early experiences laid the groundwork for his later commitment to competitive cycling.

Tadej has a younger brother, which contributed to a spirited household atmosphere. The siblings often participated in sports together, further fueling Tadej's competitive spirit and teamwork skills. His family's involvement in sports also created a culture of discipline and resilience, values that Tadej would carry with him into his cycling career.

The supportive nature of his family extended beyond just recreational activities. They provided Tadej with the necessary resources for training, from equipment to transportation to races. This encouragement was crucial, especially as Tadej began participating in local cycling competitions. His parents made sacrifices to ensure he had the opportunities to train and compete, instilling a sense of gratitude and responsibility in him.

Tadej's upbringing in Slovenia, a country with a rich cycling culture, further influenced his development. He was inspired by local cycling legends and immersed in a community that celebrated athletic achievements. This environment not only nurtured his talent but also instilled a strong sense of pride in representing his country on the international stage.

Tadej Pogačar's childhood and family background provided a solid foundation for his success as a cyclist. The values of hard work, dedication, and support from his family have been integral to his journey, helping him rise from a young boy with a bicycle to a world-class cycling champion.

Tadej Pogačar's introduction to cycling began in his early childhood, shaped by a combination of family support and a natural affinity for sports. Growing up in Komenda, Slovenia,

Tadej was exposed to cycling from a young age. His parents, recognizing his enthusiasm, encouraged him to explore the sport, often taking him on family bike rides through the beautiful Slovenian countryside. These outings were not just recreational; they fostered a love for cycling and laid the groundwork for Tadej's future in competitive racing.

At around the age of six, Tadej joined a local cycling club, which marked the official start of his journey into the world of competitive cycling. This decision opened up new opportunities for him to develop his skills and learn the fundamentals of the sport. In the supportive environment of the club, he trained alongside peers who shared his passion, allowing him to experience the camaraderie and excitement of cycling.

As he progressed, Tadej quickly distinguished himself among his peers. His talent was evident, and he began participating in local races, where he often achieved impressive results. His early experiences in competitive cycling helped him build confidence and hone his racing strategies, as he learned to navigate the challenges of each race and understand the importance of teamwork.

During this formative period, Tadej was also exposed to various cycling disciplines, including road racing and mountain biking. This diversity enriched his experience and allowed him to develop a versatile skill set. His ability to adapt to different terrains and racing styles set him apart and paved the way for his future success in road cycling.

Tadej's introduction to cycling was characterized by a blend of passion, support, and early success. The foundation built during these formative years shaped his identity as a cyclist and instilled in him a strong work ethic and determination to excel. As he moved into more competitive ranks, Tadej carried with him the lessons learned during these early days, which would ultimately guide him to become one of the most successful cyclists of his generation.

Tadej Pogačar's journey in cycling has been significantly shaped by various influences and inspirations throughout his life. Growing up in Slovenia, a country known for its stunning landscapes and rich cycling culture, Tadej was surrounded by an environment that naturally fostered his passion for the sport. From an early age, he was inspired by local cycling legends, who showcased the possibilities of success in professional cycling. Their achievements instilled in him the belief that he, too, could make his mark on the sport.

One of Tadej's most significant influences has been his family. His parents were not only supportive but also enthusiastic participants in outdoor activities, including cycling. They encouraged him to pursue his interests, providing the necessary resources and motivation to help him develop his skills. Their unwavering support during his formative years instilled in him a strong sense of determination and resilience, qualities that have been pivotal in his success as a cyclist.

Tadej's early coaches played a crucial role in his development. They recognized his potential and guided him through the early stages of his cycling career, teaching him essential techniques and strategies. Their mentorship helped him navigate the competitive landscape, shaping his understanding of racing dynamics and the importance of teamwork.

As he progressed in his career, Tadej drew inspiration from established champions in the cycling world. He admired riders like Alberto Contador and Chris Froome, whose dedication, work ethic, and ability to perform under pressure motivated him to push his limits. Watching their performances in prestigious races, especially the Tour de France, fueled his ambition to emulate their success.

Moreover, the support of his teammates at UAE Team Emirates has been invaluable. The collaborative spirit within the team has not only fostered a competitive environment but also provided Tadej with a sense of belonging. Learning from experienced riders and sharing triumphs and challenges with his teammates has enriched his experience and contributed to his growth as a cyclist.

Tadej Pogačar's influences and inspirations have come from a combination of family support, mentorship, and the achievements of cycling legends. These factors have shaped his character, instilled a sense of ambition, and guided him on his journey to becoming a world-renowned cycling champion. As he continues to inspire others with his achievements, Tadej embodies the essence of dedication, resilience, and the pursuit of excellence in the sport of cycling.

CHAPTER 2 BEGINNING OF HIS CYCLING CAREER

Tadej Pogačar's cycling career began in earnest when he joined a local cycling club in Slovenia at a young age. His initial forays into competitive racing came during his early teenage years, where he quickly made a name for himself. His natural talent, coupled with rigorous training and the support of his family and coaches, set the stage for a promising future in the sport.

As a junior cyclist, Tadej participated in various national competitions, consistently performing well and earning recognition for his abilities. His victories in local races caught the attention of talent scouts and cycling teams, paving the way for opportunities to compete at higher levels. Tadej's determination and work ethic were evident; he dedicated countless hours to training, often pushing himself to exceed his limits.

In 2016, Tadej made a significant leap by joining the Slovenian junior national team. This opportunity allowed him to compete on an international stage, facing off against some of the best young cyclists in Europe. His performances during this period were impressive; he won several junior races, including the prestigious Junior Tour of Slovenia. These victories highlighted his potential as a future star in cycling and garnered him more attention from professional teams.

The turning point in Tadej's early career came in 2019 when he signed with UAE Team Emirates, a professional cycling team competing at the highest level. This marked the beginning of his transition from junior competitions to the professional circuit. His debut season with the team was remarkable; he showcased his versatility and tenacity by winning multiple races, including the Tour of California.

His success in these early races laid the groundwork for what would be a meteoric rise in the sport. Tadej's impressive performances demonstrated his ability to compete against seasoned professionals, proving that he was more than just a promising talent—he was a force to be reckoned with.

The beginning of Tadej Pogačar's cycling career was marked by determination, hard work, and a series of successes that positioned him as one of the most exciting young talents in the cycling world. His journey from a local cycling club to professional competition exemplifies his commitment to the sport and sets the stage for the extraordinary achievements that would follow.

Tadej Pogačar's first races and competitions were instrumental in shaping his early cycling career and establishing him as a rising star in the sport. Beginning his journey at a local cycling club in Slovenia, Tadej quickly transitioned from recreational riding to competitive racing. His early participation in local events allowed him to gain invaluable experience and build his confidence on the bike.

As a junior cyclist, Tadej competed in various regional and national races, where he showcased his remarkable talent and determination. His first significant competitions included youth races across Slovenia, where he often finished at the top of the standings. These early victories not only earned him recognition within the cycling community but also fueled his ambition to pursue a professional career.

One of the defining moments of his early racing career came when he participated in the Junior Tour of Slovenia. Competing against some of the best young cyclists in the country, Tadej's impressive performance captured the attention of talent scouts and coaches. His ability to handle challenging terrains and demonstrate exceptional climbing skills set him apart from his peers, solidifying his reputation as a promising cyclist.

In 2016, Tadej was selected to represent Slovenia in international junior competitions, further elevating his profile. He competed in events such as the European Road Championships and the World Cycling Championships, where he faced off against the top young cyclists from around the globe. These experiences were pivotal for Tadej, exposing him to higher levels of competition and helping him refine his racing tactics.

His participation in these early races laid the foundation for his future success, teaching him crucial lessons about strategy, endurance, and the importance of teamwork. Tadej quickly gained a reputation for his resilience and tenacity on the bike, often pushing himself to achieve personal bests, even in challenging conditions.

Tadej Pogačar's first races and competitions marked the beginning of a remarkable journey. These experiences not only honed his skills but also instilled a deep passion for cycling, setting the stage for his transition to the professional ranks and ultimately his ascent to becoming one of the most successful cyclists of his generation.

Joining a cycling team was a pivotal moment in Tadej Pogačar's career, marking his transition from a promising junior cyclist to a professional athlete. In 2019, Pogačar signed with UAE Team Emirates, a prestigious professional cycling team known for its competitive edge and strong roster of riders. This opportunity came after a series of impressive performances in junior competitions, which showcased his remarkable talent and potential.

Joining UAE Team Emirates provided Tadej with the necessary platform to develop his skills at the highest level of the sport. The team's professional environment offered him access to world-class coaching, advanced training facilities, and the chance to race alongside seasoned professionals. This transition was crucial for his growth as an athlete, allowing him to learn from experienced teammates and absorb the nuances of professional cycling.

His first season with the team was nothing short of spectacular. Pogačar quickly made his mark by winning the Tour of California, where he claimed three stage victories and the overall title. This success was a significant milestone, demonstrating that he could compete against some of the best cyclists in the world. His impressive performance in California laid the groundwork for his future successes and solidified his status as a rising star in the sport.

Throughout the season, Tadej participated in several high-profile races, including the Vuelta a España and the Tour de France, gaining invaluable experience in elite competition. His adaptability and resilience on the bike shone through, as he navigated various terrains and challenges. The support from his team played a crucial role during this time; teammates and coaches provided guidance, helping him refine his racing strategies and manage the physical demands of professional cycling.

Pogačar's ability to integrate into the team dynamic and contribute to collective goals further demonstrated his potential. He often displayed a strong team spirit, recognizing the importance of collaboration in achieving success. This attitude not only earned him the respect of his teammates but also contributed to a positive team culture.

 joining UAE Team Emirates marked a significant turning point in Tadej Pogačar's cycling career. It provided him with the platform, resources, and support necessary to flourish as a professional cyclist. His early success with the team set the stage for an extraordinary career, showcasing his exceptional talent and determination on the world stage.

CHAPTER 3 RISE TO FAME

Tadej Pogačar's rise to fame in the cycling world has been a remarkable journey characterized by extraordinary talent, determination, and a series of breathtaking performances. His ascent began shortly after he joined UAE Team Emirates in 2019, where he quickly proved himself as one of the most promising young cyclists in the sport.

The turning point in his career came during the 2020 Tour de France, where Pogačar delivered a performance that would not only earn him the prestigious yellow jersey but also capture the hearts of cycling fans worldwide. At just 21 years old, he became the youngest rider to win the Tour since its inception in 1903. His ability to clinch victory was particularly dramatic, as he overtook fellow competitor Primož Roglič in the final time trial of the race, showcasing his exceptional climbing skills and time-trialing prowess. This remarkable achievement catapulted him into the spotlight, establishing him as a formidable force in professional cycling.

Pogačar's success in the 2020 Tour de France was not an isolated incident; it was the culmination of consistent performances throughout the season. Prior to the Tour, he had already made headlines by winning several prestigious races, including the UAE Tour and the Volta ao Algarve. His ability to dominate across diverse terrains demonstrated his versatility and marked him as a multifaceted athlete capable of excelling in various race conditions.

Following his Tour de France victory, Tadej's fame continued to grow. In 2021, he successfully defended his title, becoming the youngest rider to win the Tour twice. His performances during this edition were nothing short of spectacular, including multiple stage wins and a commanding lead in the general classification. His back-to-back victories solidified his reputation as one of the best cyclists of his generation.

Beyond his accomplishments in the Tour de France, Pogačar's rise to fame was also fueled by his charisma and approachability. He has cultivated a strong connection with fans through social media, sharing insights into his training, daily life, and personal experiences. This transparency has made him relatable and endeared him to cycling enthusiasts around the globe.

As his fame grew, Pogačar also became a key figure in promoting the sport of cycling, inspiring young athletes and capturing the attention of media outlets. His success has encouraged greater interest in cycling, particularly in Slovenia, where he has become a national hero.

Tadej Pogačar's rise to fame is a testament to his incredible talent, hard work, and resilience. From his stunning performances in prestigious races to his ability to connect with fans, he has redefined what it means to be a champion in modern cycling. As he continues to compete and achieve remarkable milestones, Tadej remains a symbol of inspiration for aspiring cyclists around the world.

Tadej Pogačar's breakthrough performances have defined his career and established him as one of the most exceptional talents in professional cycling. His ascent to prominence was marked by a series of remarkable results that showcased his versatility, determination, and sheer ability to excel in high-pressure situations.

One of the most significant breakthroughs in Pogačar's career came during the 2020 Tour de France. As a relatively young and inexperienced rider, he faced seasoned competitors, but his performance was nothing short of extraordinary. In a dramatic turn of events, he claimed the yellow jersey on the penultimate stage, overtaking Primož Roglič, who had been leading the race. Pogačar's victory in the final time trial solidified his status as the youngest winner of the Tour de France in over a century, a feat that not only earned him acclaim but also changed the trajectory of his career.

Pogačar also won the white jersey for the best young rider and the polka dot jersey for the king of the mountains, making him the first rider since 1983 to win all three jerseys in the same Tour. This historic achievement showcased his all-around capabilities, from climbing to time-trialing, and cemented his reputation as a multifaceted cyclist.

Following his Tour de France triumph, Pogačar continued to deliver impressive performances throughout the 2021 season. One of the standout moments was his victory in the 2021 Tour de France, where he defended his title with an authoritative display. He won multiple stages and displayed dominance in both the mountains and time trials, proving that his first victory was not a fluke but rather the beginning of a sustained period of excellence. His ability to maintain composure and deliver under pressure in this highly competitive environment reinforced his status as a cycling superstar.

Beyond the Tour de France, Pogačar's breakout performances included significant wins in other prestigious races. In 2020, he secured victories in the UAE Tour, where he won three stages and the overall classification, showcasing his capacity to dominate in multi-stage events. He also achieved success in the Volta ao Algarve, where he claimed the overall title and a stage victory, further highlighting his rising status within the sport.

In 2022, he continued to impress with a series of wins, including the Tour of Flanders, one of cycling's five Monuments, which demonstrated his ability to compete in diverse race formats, from Grand Tours to one-day classics.

Pogačar's breakthrough performances have not only propelled him into the limelight but have also inspired a new generation of cyclists. His resilience, tactical acumen, and relentless pursuit of excellence serve as a blueprint for aspiring athletes in the sport. As he continues to achieve remarkable milestones, Tadej Pogačar remains a defining figure in modern cycling, a testament to the potential that dedication and talent can unlock.

Joining UAE Team Emirates was a pivotal moment in Tadej Pogačar's cycling career, marking his transition from promising junior cyclist to professional athlete on an elite stage. After showcasing remarkable talent and determination in local and junior competitions, Pogačar caught the attention of the team's management and was signed in 2019. This opportunity represented a significant leap, as UAE Team Emirates is one of the most prestigious cycling teams in the world, competing at the highest levels of the sport, including the UCI World Tour.

From the outset, joining UAE Team Emirates provided Tadej with access to top-tier coaching, advanced training facilities, and a support network of experienced riders. The professional environment of the team was instrumental in refining his skills, as he was able to train alongside seasoned cyclists who had extensive experience in Grand Tours and classic races. This exposure allowed him to learn the intricacies of professional racing, from developing race strategies to understanding the importance of teamwork.

Tadej's debut season with UAE Team Emirates was remarkable. He quickly established himself as a formidable competitor, winning multiple races and earning recognition for his versatility. His performance in the UAE Tour, where he won three stages and the overall classification, served as a clear signal of his potential. This early success helped him gain confidence and validate his decision to join the team.

The turning point in his career, however, came just months after his initial signing when he competed in the 2020 Tour de France. As a young rider, Tadej faced experienced competitors but quickly made headlines with his exceptional performance.

He not only won the yellow jersey, becoming the youngest winner in the race's history, but also claimed the white and polka dot jerseys. This historic achievement put him squarely in the spotlight and solidified his position as one of the sport's brightest stars.

Throughout his time with UAE Team Emirates, Pogačar has shown remarkable growth as an athlete. The team's emphasis on fostering young talent and promoting a collaborative environment allowed him to flourish. Teammates and coaches provided guidance, helping him refine his racing techniques and navigate the demands of professional cycling.

 joining UAE Team Emirates marked a transformative chapter in Tadej Pogačar's career. The team provided him with the platform, resources, and support needed to develop into a world-class cyclist. His subsequent performances, especially in prestigious races like the Tour de France, showcased his talent and determination, setting the stage for what has become an extraordinary career in professional cycling. As he continues to compete and achieve new milestones, Pogačar remains a key figure within UAE Team Emirates and a prominent name in the world of cycling.

CHAPTER 4 MAJOR ACHIEVEMENTS

Tadej Pogačar's cycling career is marked by a series of remarkable achievements that have established him as one of the foremost cyclists of his generation. His accomplishments span various prestigious races, showcasing his versatility, skill, and competitive spirit. Here are some of his major achievements

2020: Pogačar made history by winning the Tour de France at just 21 years old, becoming the youngest winner of the race. He clinched the yellow jersey in a dramatic final time trial, overtaking his rival Primož Roglič. He also won the white jersey for the best young rider and the polka dot jersey for the king of the mountains, becoming the first rider to win all three jerseys in a single Tour since 1983.

2021: He successfully defended his title, demonstrating his dominance by winning multiple stages and solidifying his status as a top contender in professional cycling

Pogačar won the overall classification of the UAE Tour in 2020, where he secured three stage victories. This success marked a strong start to his professional career and demonstrated his ability to compete in multi-stage events.

In 2021, he won La Flèche Wallonne, one of cycling's classic races. His victory at this prestigious event showcased his strength and tactical acumen in hilly terrain, further establishing him as a versatile rider.

Pogačar clinched victory in the 2021 Giro di Lombardia, one of cycling's five Monuments. This win highlighted his ability to excel in one-day races, particularly those that feature challenging climbs and technical descents.

He won the overall classification of the Volta ao Algarve in 2020, adding to his growing list of achievements and demonstrating his prowess in stage racing.

In 2022, Pogačar triumphed in the Tour of Flanders, becoming one of the few riders to win both a Monument and a Grand Tour in the same season. This victory showcased his ability to compete in a variety of race formats.

Pogačar represented Slovenia at the UCI Road World Championships, earning medals and showcasing his talent on an international stage. His performances contributed to Slovenia's growing reputation in the cycling world.

He has also claimed several national titles in Slovenia, further establishing his dominance in his home country.

Pogačar consistently ranks among the top cyclists in Grand Tours, demonstrating his ability to compete in three-week races and perform exceptionally in challenging conditions.

Tadej Pogačar's achievements reflect his exceptional talent, dedication, and relentless pursuit of excellence in cycling. As he continues to compete at the highest level, his growing list of accolades cements his legacy as one of the greatest cyclists of his generation and an inspiration for aspiring athletes worldwide.

Winning the Tour de France was a monumental achievement in Tadej Pogačar's cycling career, marking him as one of the sport's elite athletes at just 21 years old. His first victory in the 2020 edition of the race was not only a personal triumph but also a historic milestone in cycling history, as he became the youngest winner of the Tour since its inception in 1903. The journey to this prestigious win was marked by exceptional performances, strategic racing, and remarkable resilience.

Pogačar entered the 2020 Tour de France as a relatively young competitor, but he quickly demonstrated his prowess in the early stages of the race. From the outset, he showcased his ability to navigate through the challenging terrains of the French countryside, earning crucial time bonuses with strong finishes. His consistent performances built momentum and established him as a formidable contender.

The defining moment of Pogačar's Tour de France victory came on the penultimate stage, a grueling time trial that would ultimately decide the overall classification. As he prepared for the stage, he faced a significant challenge, trailing the then-leader, Primož Roglič, by a substantial margin. However, Pogačar approached the time trial with a strategic mindset and an unyielding determination. He executed a flawless ride, demonstrating his exceptional time-trialing abilities, and remarkably overtook Roglič in the final moments of the stage.

This dramatic turnaround not only secured him the yellow jersey but also showcased his strength, focus, and racing intelligence. His ability to perform under pressure, particularly in a high-stakes environment like the Tour de France, underscored his potential as a future champion. By claiming the yellow jersey, Pogačar also became the first Slovenian rider to win the Tour, a moment of national pride that resonated deeply with fans in his home country.

Pogačar's outstanding performance throughout the race earned him the white jersey for the best young rider and the polka dot jersey for the king of the mountains. This unique achievement highlighted his versatility and dominance across various race categories, further solidifying his legacy in cycling history. He became the first rider to win all three jerseys in the same Tour, a feat that underscored his multifaceted skills as a cyclist.

Winning the Tour de France transformed Pogačar's career overnight, propelling him into the international spotlight and making him a household name in the sport. His victory not only reflected his hard work and dedication but also served as an inspiration to aspiring cyclists around the world. Following the Tour, Pogačar continued to compete at a high level, defending his title in 2021 and showcasing his commitment to maintaining excellence in the sport.

Tadej Pogačar's triumph at the Tour de France was a culmination of talent, preparation, and mental fortitude. It established him as one of the premier cyclists of his generation and set the stage for future successes in his already illustrious career. The impact of his victory resonates beyond the race itself, inspiring a new wave of cycling enthusiasts and athletes who aspire to follow in his footsteps.

Tadej Pogačar's prowess in cycling extends beyond his remarkable triumphs in the Tour de France; he has also achieved significant victories in other Grand Tours, solidifying his status as one of the top riders in professional cycling. His success in these prestigious multi-stage races demonstrates his versatility, endurance, and strategic racing capabilities.

Following his historic win in the 2020 Tour de France, Pogačar continued to compete at an elite level, showcasing his talent in various Grand Tours. One of his most notable victories came in the 2021 Tour de France, where he successfully defended his title. Pogačar dominated the race from the beginning, showcasing his exceptional climbing abilities and time-trialing skills. He won multiple stages and consistently finished in the top positions, securing his place as the overall winner once again. This victory not only made him the youngest rider to win the Tour twice but also cemented his reputation as a dominant force in the cycling world.

Pogačar also claimed victory in the 2021 Vuelta a España. This Grand Tour, known for its challenging routes and mountainous terrains, presented a unique test of endurance and strategy. Pogačar's performance in the Vuelta was impressive; he showcased his ability to compete across various terrains, winning crucial stages and maintaining a strong overall position. His adaptability and resilience were key factors in his success, allowing him to emerge as the overall winner of the Vuelta.

Pogačar's victories in Grand Tours reflect not only his physical capabilities but also his tactical acumen. He has demonstrated a keen understanding of race dynamics, often positioning himself strategically to gain advantages over his competitors. His ability to thrive in high-pressure situations, particularly in the final stages of races, sets him apart from many of his peers.

The impact of Pogačar's Grand Tour victories has reverberated throughout the cycling community. As a young cyclist achieving remarkable success on such a grand scale, he has inspired a new generation of athletes. His approach to training, dedication to the sport, and willingness to push boundaries have made him a role model for aspiring cyclists worldwide.

Tadej Pogačar's Grand Tour victories extend beyond his achievements In the Tour de France, encompassing remarkable performances in events like the Vuelta a España. His ability to excel in multi-stage races, coupled with his strategic racing style, positions him as one of the premier cyclists in the sport today. As he continues to compete and strive for new achievements, Pogačar's legacy in professional cycling is only set to grow, making him a significant figure in the history of the sport.

Tadej Pogačar's career is adorned with numerous championships and awards that reflect his extraordinary talent and significant contributions to professional cycling. His achievements span multiple prestigious events, showcasing his versatility as a rider and his ability to perform at the highest level.

One of Pogačar's most notable accolades is his two Tour de France victories, first in 2020 and then in 2021. These wins not only solidified his status as one of the top cyclists of his generation but also made him the youngest rider to win the Tour multiple times. Additionally, during both editions of the race, he earned the coveted polka dot jersey for the best climber and the white jersey for the best young rider, highlighting his all-around capabilities.

In addition to his success in the Tour de France, Pogačar has claimed titles in several other significant races. His victories in the UAE Tour, where he won the overall classification and several stages in 2020, underscored his talent in stage racing. He also triumphed in the Volta ao Algarve in 2020, further establishing his reputation as a formidable competitor in various terrains and conditions.

Pogačar's impressive performance in one-day races has also garnered him acclaim. His victory in the prestigious La Flèche Wallonne in 2021 showcased his ability to excel in hilly and challenging courses. He followed this success with a win in the 2021 Giro di Lombardia, another classic race that affirmed his versatility and strength as a cyclist.

His accomplishments have not gone unnoticed, as Pogačar has received numerous awards and honors from the cycling community. He was named the Slovenian Sportsman of the Year for his outstanding performances and contributions to the sport, and he has been recognized by the Union Cycliste Internationale (UCI) for his achievements.

His impact on the sport extends beyond individual awards; Pogačar's presence in the cycling world has helped elevate the profile of Slovenian cycling on the international stage. His victories have inspired a new generation of cyclists and contributed to a growing interest in the sport within Slovenia.

Tadej Pogačar's championships and awards are a testament to his remarkable talent, hard work, and dedication to cycling. His impressive list of accolades reflects not only his individual achievements but also his role in promoting the sport and inspiring future athletes. As he continues to compete at the highest level, Pogačar's legacy in professional cycling will undoubtedly grow, making him a significant figure in the history of the sport.

CHAPTER 5 RACING STYLE AND TECHNIQUES

Tadej Pogačar's racing style and techniques have played a crucial role in his success as a professional cyclist, distinguishing him as one of the most talented riders in the sport. His approach to racing is characterized by a blend of tactical acumen, exceptional physical abilities, and a keen understanding of race dynamics, allowing him to excel in a variety of competitive settings.

One of the hallmarks of Pogačar's racing style is his versatility. He is proficient in multiple disciplines within cycling, including climbing, time trialing, and one-day races. This adaptability enables him to perform well across different race formats, whether in mountainous terrain, flat stages, or time trials. Pogačar's ability to shift gears and adjust his strategy based on the specific demands of each race makes him a formidable competitor.

Pogačar is particularly renowned for his climbing prowess. His technique on ascents combines strength, endurance, and an efficient pedaling style. He has an innate ability to gauge his effort, allowing him to conserve energy during long climbs while maintaining a competitive pace. His explosive power enables him to make decisive attacks, often leaving rivals behind on steep gradients. This skill was prominently displayed during his Tour de France victories, where he consistently outperformed other climbers in challenging mountain stages.

In addition to his climbing abilities, Pogačar is an exceptional time trialist. His aerodynamic position on the bike and strong pedal stroke contribute to his speed and efficiency during individual time trials. Pogačar's time trialing technique emphasizes a balance between power output and energy conservation, allowing him to maximize his performance over long distances. His memorable performance in the 2020 Tour de France time trial, where he overtook the race leader to claim the yellow jersey, showcased his skill in this discipline.

Pogačar's racing style is also marked by his tactical awareness and intelligence. He possesses a deep understanding of race dynamics and can anticipate the moves of his competitors. This foresight allows him to make strategic decisions during critical moments, whether that means launching an attack, following rivals, or conserving energy for later stages. His ability to read the race and adapt his strategy has often given him the upper hand against seasoned competitors.

While Pogačar is an outstanding individual performer, he also values teamwork in his racing approach. He works closely with his teammates from UAE Team Emirates, relying on their support during key moments of races. His collaborative style includes utilizing teammates to shield him from wind, help navigate the peloton, and provide crucial assistance during climbs and sprints. This synergy allows him to focus on his performance while relying on his team's strengths.

Another essential aspect of Pogačar's racing style is his mental resilience. He approaches challenges with a composed mindset, often exhibiting calmness during high-pressure situations. This mental fortitude enables him to stay focused and execute his race plan effectively, even in the face of adversity. His ability to bounce back from setbacks or respond to the unexpected is a testament to his competitive spirit.

Tadej Pogačar's racing style and techniques are defined by his versatility, exceptional climbing and time trialing skills, tactical awareness, teamwork, and mental resilience. These elements combine to create a formidable cyclist capable of excelling in various racing environments. As he continues to compete at the highest levels, Pogačar's innovative approach and mastery of the sport serve as an inspiration to both his peers and aspiring cyclists worldwide.

Tadej Pogačar's strengths as a cyclist have made him a dominant force in professional cycling, setting him apart from his peers and establishing him as one of the best riders of his generation. His combination of physical abilities, mental toughness, and strategic insight has allowed him to excel in various competitive environments. Here are some key strengths that define his cycling prowess:

Pogačar's exceptional climbing skills are among his most significant strengths. He possesses a remarkable power-to-weight ratio, enabling him to ascend steep gradients with efficiency and speed. His ability to accelerate on climbs allows him to break away from competitors, making him a formidable presence in mountainous stages of races such as the Tour de France. Pogačar's technique, including smooth pedaling and strategic pacing, further enhances his performance in high-altitude conditions.

Pogačar is also an outstanding time trialist. His aerodynamic position and strong cadence contribute to his ability to maintain high speeds over individual time trials. He combines power output with energy conservation, enabling him to perform exceptionally well in time-trial stages, which often prove crucial in multi-stage races. His performance during the time trial in the 2020 Tour de France, where he clinched the yellow jersey, highlights his strength in this discipline.

One of Pogačar's most defining strengths is his versatility. He is capable of excelling in various types of races, including stage races, one-day classics, and flat terrains. His adaptability allows him to compete effectively in different conditions, whether it be climbing in the mountains or sprinting on flat roads. This versatility makes him a well-rounded rider and a consistent threat in any race format.

Pogačar's tactical acumen is another significant asset. He possesses a keen understanding of race dynamics, allowing him to anticipate the moves of his competitors and respond accordingly. His ability to devise strategies that leverage his strengths while exploiting the weaknesses of others gives him a competitive edge. This strategic insight often leads to well-timed attacks or defensive moves, particularly in critical stages of races.

Pogačar's mental toughness is evident in his approach to competition. He maintains composure under pressure, enabling him to stay focused during challenging situations. His resilience allows him to overcome setbacks, whether it's dealing with a difficult stage or a challenging competitor. This mental fortitude not only helps him in high-stakes moments but also inspires confidence in his teammates.

While Pogačar is an exceptional individual performer, he also values collaboration within his team, UAE Team Emirates. His ability to work effectively with teammates enhances his performance, as he can rely on them for support during key moments of races. Whether it's receiving help in the peloton or strategizing together during stages, this teamwork is crucial in achieving success in multi-stage events.

Pogačar's commitment to rigorous training and preparation is a foundational strength. He approaches his training regimen with discipline and dedication, continually seeking ways to improve his performance. His ability to adapt training techniques to address specific goals or challenges has contributed to his ongoing success.

Tadej Pogačar's strengths as a cyclist encompass his climbing ability, time trialing skills, versatility, tactical intelligence, mental resilience, collaboration with teammates, and commitment to training. Together, these strengths create a formidable competitor capable of achieving remarkable success in the world of professional cycling. As he continues to push the boundaries of his abilities, Pogačar's strengths will undoubtedly contribute to his legacy in the sport.

Tadej Pogačar's success in professional cycling can be attributed not only to his physical abilities but also to his astute race strategies. His approach to racing is characterized by a combination of tactical awareness, adaptability, and an understanding of both his strengths and the dynamics of his competitors. Here are some key strategies that define Pogačar's racing style:

Pogačar possesses a keen ability to read the race and assess the strengths and weaknesses of his competitors. He often observes how rivals react to certain situations, such as climbs or sprints, allowing him to formulate a plan based on their behavior. By understanding the capabilities of his opponents, Pogačar can time his attacks more effectively.

One of Pogačar's hallmark strategies is launching attacks at pivotal moments during races. Whether on steep climbs or during crucial points in a stage, he knows when to make decisive moves to gain an advantage. His timing is often impeccable, allowing him to catch competitors off guard and create gaps that can be difficult to close.

Pogačar recognizes the importance of teamwork in achieving success in multi-stage races. He collaborates closely with his teammates from UAE Team Emirates, utilizing their strengths to enhance his performance. This includes having teammates shield him from wind, help navigate the peloton, and provide support during climbs. Effective communication within the team allows for strategic planning and execution during critical race moments.

Pogačar is adept at managing his energy levels throughout a race. He strategically positions himself in the peloton to avoid excessive effort during less challenging segments, conserving energy for decisive moments. This calculated approach enables him to maintain a high level of performance during crucial climbs and sprints, ultimately contributing to his success in securing victories.

Pogačar's versatility allows him to adapt his racing strategy based on varying weather and terrain conditions. He can adjust his approach during wet or challenging conditions, focusing on maintaining stability and control while others may struggle. His ability to excel in diverse environments—whether mountainous, flat, or windy—provides him with an advantage over less adaptable competitors.

Pogačar's time trialing skills are integral to his overall strategy in stage races. He often approaches time trial stages with the goal of gaining crucial time over competitors. His emphasis on a strong performance in time trials can significantly alter the overall standings, allowing him to create gaps that can be defended in subsequent stages.

Mental resilience is a core element of Pogačar's race strategy. He prepares himself to handle pressure and challenges during races, maintaining focus and composure in high-stakes situations. His mental strength allows him to execute strategies effectively, even when faced with adversity or unexpected developments.

Pogačar is known for his ability to adapt his strategies on the fly. While he may enter a race with a specific plan, he remains open to changing tactics based on the race's progression. This flexibility allows him to respond effectively to shifts in the race dynamics, such as changes in competitors' tactics or unexpected obstacles.

In stage races, Pogačar often identifies specific stages that align with his strengths, such as mountain stages or time trials. By targeting these key stages, he can focus his efforts on maximizing his performance where he knows he can gain the most advantage, ultimately contributing to his overall standing in the race.

Tadej Pogačar's key strategies in races highlight his tactical intelligence, adaptability, and collaborative spirit. By effectively assessing competitors, utilizing team support, conserving energy, and adapting to various conditions, Pogačar has established himself as a dominant force in professional cycling. His ability to implement these strategies with precision has led to remarkable successes and continues to inspire cyclists and fans around the world.

CHAPTER 6 LIFE OUTSIDE CYCLING

Tadej Pogačar's life outside cycling reflects his multifaceted personality and interests beyond the competitive realm of professional sports. While he dedicates a significant portion of his time to training, racing, and honing his cycling skills, he also engages in various activities and pursuits that showcase his character and values.

Family plays an essential role in Pogačar's life. He has a close relationship with his family, who have supported him throughout his cycling journey. He often expresses gratitude for their encouragement and guidance, emphasizing the importance of a strong support system in achieving his goals. Despite his rising fame, he maintains a down-to-earth attitude and values quality time spent with loved ones.

Outside of cycling, Pogačar has a deep appreciation for nature and the outdoors. Growing up in Slovenia, a country renowned for its stunning landscapes, he developed a love for outdoor activities beyond biking. Hiking and exploring natural environments provide him with relaxation and a break from the rigors of training and competition. This connection to nature also aligns with his commitment to sustainability and environmental conservation.

Pogačar's passion for sports extends beyond cycling. He enjoys participating in various physical activities that complement his training regimen. Activities like running, hiking, and strength training contribute to his overall fitness and endurance. His enthusiasm for fitness underscores his commitment to maintaining a healthy lifestyle, which is crucial for any professional athlete.

Pogačar is actively involved in charitable initiatives, demonstrating his desire to give back to the community. He participates in events that support youth sports programs and promote physical activity among young people. By advocating for cycling and fitness, he hopes to inspire the next generation of athletes and encourage them to pursue their passions.

As a prominent figure in professional cycling, Pogačar enjoys engaging with his fans and sharing his journey with them. He often utilizes social media platforms to connect with supporters, providing insights into his training, races, and personal life. This engagement fosters a sense of community and allows fans to follow his progress as he navigates the challenges of professional cycling.

Pogačar also has a keen interest in culture and enjoys exploring different aspects of life beyond sports. He appreciates music, art, and literature, often seeking inspiration from various cultural influences. This appreciation for the arts adds depth to his personality and reflects a well-rounded individual who values experiences beyond athletic achievement.

While Pogačar remains focused on his cycling career, he also contemplates his future beyond the sport. He recognizes the importance of life after cycling and expresses interest in pursuing education or other endeavors that allow him to contribute positively to society. This forward-thinking mindset showcases his maturity and understanding of the importance of balancing professional success with personal development.

Tadej Pogačar's life outside cycling is marked by a rich tapestry of family, nature, community involvement, and personal interests. His dedication to fitness, commitment to charitable work, and engagement with fans reflect a well-rounded individual who values relationships and experiences beyond the cycling world. As he continues to achieve remarkable success in his cycling career, Pogačar's character and values shine through, making him not only a champion on the bike but also an inspiring role model off of it.

Tadej Pogačar's interests and hobbies reveal a well-rounded individual who values experiences beyond his professional cycling career. While he dedicates much of his time to training and competition, he also engages in various activities that reflect his personality and passions.

One of Pogačar's primary interests is exploring the great outdoors. Growing up in Slovenia, a country known for its breathtaking landscapes, he developed a deep appreciation for nature. Hiking and spending time in the mountains provide him with a sense of tranquility and an opportunity to disconnect from the pressures of racing. Whether it's scaling steep trails or simply enjoying the beauty of the natural environment, Pogačar finds solace and inspiration in these outdoor pursuits. This connection to nature not only serves as a means of relaxation but also aligns with his commitment to environmental conservation, highlighting his respect for the world around him.

In addition to his love for nature, Pogačar has a keen interest in sports beyond cycling. He enjoys participating in various physical activities that complement his training regimen, such as running and strength training. These activities not only help him maintain his fitness but also provide a welcome break from the monotony of cycling. His enthusiasm for sports reflects a broader commitment to a healthy lifestyle and physical well-being, reinforcing his dedication to personal growth and athletic development.

Pogačar also values community and often engages in charitable initiatives. He is passionate about promoting youth sports and encouraging young people to pursue their athletic interests. By participating in events and activities that support these causes, he aims to inspire the next generation of athletes. This commitment to giving back showcases his desire to make a positive impact in the lives of others and highlights his belief in the importance of physical activity for overall well-being.

Social media plays an essential role in Pogačar's life, allowing him to connect with fans and share his experiences. He enjoys engaging with his followers, providing insights into his training routines, race preparations, and personal reflections. This interaction fosters a sense of community and enables him to maintain a close connection with his supporters, who follow his journey both on and off the bike. His willingness to share personal moments further humanizes him, making him relatable to fans who admire his achievements.

Pogačar has a strong appreciation for culture and enjoys exploring various forms of art, music, and literature. He often finds inspiration in different cultural experiences, which enrich his life outside of cycling. This engagement with the arts showcases his curiosity and highlights the importance he places on diverse experiences, emphasizing that he is not solely defined by his athletic accomplishments.

Looking to the future, Pogačar contemplates life beyond cycling, recognizing the significance of personal growth and education. He expresses interest in pursuing opportunities that allow him to contribute positively to society after his cycling career. This forward-thinking mindset demonstrates his maturity and understanding of the importance of balancing professional success with personal development.

Tadej Pogačar's interests and hobbies reflect a multifaceted individual who values nature, sports, community involvement, cultural experiences, and personal growth. While he is dedicated to his cycling career, his diverse interests and commitment to giving back to others make him an inspiring figure both within and outside the realm of professional sports. Through his passions, Pogačar showcases a well-rounded character that resonates with fans and aspiring athletes alike.

Tadej Pogačar's contributions to the community extend beyond his impressive achievements in professional cycling; they reflect his commitment to making a positive impact on the lives of others. Recognizing the influence he has as a prominent athlete, Pogačar actively engages in various initiatives aimed at supporting youth and promoting healthy lifestyles.

One of the central aspects of Pogačar's community involvement is his passion for encouraging young athletes. He participates in events and programs that aim to inspire the next generation of cyclists and sports enthusiasts. By sharing his experiences and insights, he motivates young people to pursue their dreams in sports, emphasizing the importance of dedication, hard work, and perseverance. His presence at these events serves not only as a source of inspiration but also as a reminder that success is attainable through commitment and resilience.

Pogačar's philanthropic efforts also extend to promoting physical activity and a healthy lifestyle among youth. He understands the significance of sport in fostering discipline, teamwork, and a sense of belonging, and he actively advocates for youth sports programs. By collaborating with local organizations and participating in community events, he helps raise awareness about the benefits of physical fitness and the importance of engaging young people in sports.

Pogačar's involvement in charitable initiatives showcases his desire to give back to the community. He supports various causes, particularly those focused on health and well-being. This includes participating in fundraising events and charity rides aimed at raising money for local charities and non-profit organizations. Through these efforts, he contributes to improving the quality of life for individuals and families in need, demonstrating his commitment to social responsibility.

In addition to his direct involvement with youth and charitable organizations, Pogačar uses his platform as a professional athlete to advocate for broader social issues. He emphasizes the importance of environmental sustainability and conservation, raising awareness about the impact of climate change and encouraging others to take action. His commitment to environmental causes reflects a holistic approach to community engagement, recognizing that the well-being of individuals is interconnected with the health of the planet.

Pogačar also engages with his fans and the broader public through social media, where he shares messages of encouragement and positivity. By communicating with his followers, he fosters a sense of community among those who look up to him as a role model. His interactions not only humanize him as an athlete but also create a supportive environment where fans feel inspired to pursue their passions and stay active.

Tadej Pogačar's contributions to the community highlight his dedication to inspiring youth, promoting healthy lifestyles, and giving back to those in need. Through his active involvement in charitable initiatives, advocacy for social causes, and engagement with fans, he exemplifies the qualities of a responsible athlete who seeks to make a meaningful difference. Pogačar's commitment to community engagement not only enhances his legacy as a champion cyclist but also positions him as an inspiring figure who motivates others to create positive change in their own lives and communities.

Tadej Pogačar's personal life and relationships provide a glimpse into the man behind the athlete. While he is widely recognized for his incredible achievements in cycling, his life outside the sport reveals a grounded individual with strong familial ties, friendships, and a sense of community.

At the core of Pogačar's personal life is his close-knit family. He was born and raised in a supportive household in Slovenia, where his parents encouraged his passions from an early age. This foundational support has been instrumental in shaping his character and guiding him through the challenges of a professional sports career. He often expresses gratitude for his family's unwavering belief in him, crediting them for instilling values of hard work, humility, and perseverance. Pogačar frequently shares moments with his family on social media, showcasing the importance of these relationships in his life.

In addition to his family, Pogačar has cultivated meaningful friendships within the cycling community and beyond. His relationships with fellow cyclists, team members, and coaches play a crucial role in his professional journey. These connections provide a support network that helps him navigate the highs and lows of competitive racing. He often emphasizes the camaraderie among cyclists, highlighting how shared experiences—both on and off the bike—forge lasting bonds.

Romantically, Pogačar has been linked to fellow athletes and public figures. His relationship is characterized by mutual support and understanding, allowing both partners to pursue their respective passions while maintaining a strong connection. Pogačar values the balance between his professional obligations and personal life, recognizing the importance of having a supportive partner who understands the demands of being a professional athlete.

Beyond family and romantic relationships, Pogačar actively engages with his fans and the broader community. He uses social media platforms to connect with supporters, sharing not only his racing experiences but also snippets of his everyday life. This openness fosters a sense of community and allows fans to feel more connected to him as a person, not just as a cyclist. His approachable demeanor and willingness to engage with followers contribute to his popularity and relatability.

Pogačar's personal life also reflects his commitment to maintaining a healthy work-life balance. While he dedicates significant time to training and competition, he makes a conscious effort to unwind and enjoy leisure activities. His love for nature, outdoor adventures, and various sports helps him recharge and find joy outside of cycling. These interests contribute to his overall well-being and enable him to approach challenges with a refreshed perspective.

Tadej Pogačar's personal life and relationships paint a picture of a grounded and relatable individual. His strong family ties, meaningful friendships, and supportive romantic relationship provide a foundation for his success in cycling. By engaging with fans and maintaining a healthy balance between his professional and personal life, Pogačar exemplifies the qualities of a champion both on and off the bike. His authenticity and commitment to fostering connections with those around him further enhance his appeal as an athlete and role model.

CHAPTER 7 LEGACY AND IMPACT

Tadej Pogačar's legacy and impact on the world of cycling extend far beyond his impressive race results. As one of the most prominent athletes of his generation, Pogačar has already established himself as a transformative figure in the sport, inspiring both current and aspiring cyclists through his achievements, character, and commitment to the cycling community.

Pogačar's rise to fame has introduced a new era in professional cycling. His remarkable accomplishments, including multiple Tour de France victories and grand tour triumphs, have not only set high standards for competitive excellence but have also captured the imagination of fans worldwide. His ability to dominate in various race formats—from one-day classics to multi-stage tours—demonstrates his versatility and commitment to the sport. By consistently performing at the highest level, Pogačar has become a symbol of what dedication, hard work, and talent can achieve, inspiring countless young athletes to pursue their dreams in cycling.

Pogačar's impact is felt beyond the competitive arena. He represents a new generation of athletes who prioritize both performance and environmental awareness. As a strong advocate for sustainability, he uses his platform to raise awareness about climate change and encourages fans and fellow athletes to adopt eco-friendly practices. This commitment to the environment resonates with a growing audience that values social responsibility and reflects a shift in how athletes engage with broader societal issues. Pogačar's influence in promoting sustainability highlights the potential for sports figures to drive positive change and inspire action within their communities.

Pogačar has significantly contributed to youth sports development. His involvement in various initiatives aimed at inspiring young cyclists and promoting healthy lifestyles showcases his dedication to nurturing the next generation. By participating in community events and sharing his experiences, he fosters a supportive environment that encourages young athletes to pursue their passions. Pogačar's willingness to mentor and inspire the youth further solidifies his role as a positive influence, emphasizing the importance of sportsmanship, teamwork, and perseverance.

Pogačar's approachability and authenticity have endeared him to fans, making him a relatable figure in the cycling world. He actively engages with supporters through social media, sharing insights into his training, races, and personal life. This transparency creates a strong connection with his audience, allowing fans to feel personally invested in his journey. His relatability and down-to-earth demeanor make him a role model not only for aspiring cyclists but for anyone seeking to overcome challenges and achieve their goals.

As Pogačar continues to excel in his cycling career, his legacy will undoubtedly evolve. He stands poised to leave an indelible mark on the sport, one characterized by extraordinary accomplishments, a commitment to sustainability, and a dedication to uplifting others. Future generations of cyclists will undoubtedly look to him as a source of inspiration, drawing lessons from his success and approach to life.

Tadej Pogačar's legacy and impact extend far beyond his accolades as a cyclist. He embodies the values of dedication, environmental stewardship, and community engagement. Through his achievements and character, Pogačar is not just shaping the future of cycling but also inspiring positive change within society. His legacy will serve as a testament to the profound influence that athletes can have on their sport and the world around them, encouraging future generations to dream big and act responsibly.

Tadej Pogačar's influence on young cyclists is profound and multifaceted, resonating with aspiring athletes who look to him as a role model and source of inspiration. His journey from a young enthusiast in Slovenia to a world-renowned cycling champion serves as a powerful narrative that encourages youth to pursue their passions, embrace hard work, and believe in their potential.

One of the most significant ways Pogačar influences young cyclists is through his exceptional achievements in the sport. His victories in prestigious races like the Tour de France and other grand tours showcase the possibilities that come with dedication, discipline, and resilience. By witnessing his success, young cyclists realize that greatness is achievable with commitment and effort. Pogačar's accomplishments serve as a tangible reminder that talent combined with hard work can lead to remarkable outcomes, motivating young athletes to strive for excellence in their own pursuits.

Pogačar's relatable personality further enhances his impact. Unlike many elite athletes who may seem distant or unapproachable, he engages openly with fans and followers on social media. By sharing glimpses of his training, personal life, and experiences, he creates a sense of connection with young cyclists. This transparency allows them to see that even champions face challenges, setbacks, and moments of self-doubt. Pogačar's willingness to share his journey encourages young athletes to embrace their struggles and view them as part of the path to success.

Pogačar actively participates in youth-oriented events and initiatives aimed at promoting cycling among young people. He often attends community cycling events, clinics, and youth races, where he interacts with budding cyclists, shares his insights, and offers encouragement. His presence at these events not only inspires young athletes but also emphasizes the importance of community and camaraderie in sports. By engaging with the next generation directly, he fosters a supportive environment that nurtures their passion for cycling and encourages them to pursue their dreams.

Pogačar's emphasis on sportsmanship and fair play also resonates with young cyclists. He consistently demonstrates respect for his competitors and the cycling community, promoting values that extend beyond winning. His commitment to integrity and teamwork serves as a model for aspiring athletes, reinforcing the idea that success in sports is not just about personal achievements but also about uplifting others and contributing positively to the sport.

Pogačar's advocacy for health and well-being plays a crucial role in influencing young cyclists. He promotes the importance of maintaining a healthy lifestyle through physical activity, balanced nutrition, and mental wellness. By emphasizing these values, he encourages young athletes to prioritize their overall well-being, fostering a holistic approach to cycling that extends beyond just training and competition.

Lastly, Pogačar's dedication to environmental sustainability adds another layer to his influence. As he champions eco-friendly practices within the cycling community, he instills a sense of responsibility in young athletes to consider the broader impact of their actions. This advocacy for environmental awareness not only encourages young cyclists to be conscious of their ecological footprint but also empowers them to become advocates for positive change in their own communities.

Tadej Pogačar's influence on young cyclists is profound, driven by his remarkable achievements, relatable personality, and commitment to sportsmanship, health, and sustainability. Through his actions and interactions, he inspires the next generation to pursue their passions, embrace challenges, and foster a sense of community within the sport. Pogačar's legacy will continue to shape the aspirations of young athletes, encouraging them to dream big, work hard, and contribute positively to the cycling world and society at large.

Tadej Pogačar's contributions to the sport of cycling are significant and multifaceted, transcending his remarkable race victories. As one of the leading figures in modern cycling, his impact is felt not only through his performance on the bike but also through his engagement with the cycling community, promotion of the sport, and advocacy for sustainable practices.

One of Pogačar's most notable contributions is his extraordinary success in major competitions, particularly his triumphs at the Tour de France, where he became the youngest winner in over a century. His ability to dominate in various race formats has set new benchmarks for excellence, inspiring a generation of cyclists to aspire to similar achievements. By consistently pushing the limits of performance, Pogačar elevates the level of competition, prompting his peers and upcoming riders to enhance their training regimens and strategies.

Pogačar has also played a pivotal role in redefining the standards of versatility in cycling. His proficiency in climbing, time trials, and flat stages showcases a well-rounded skill set that challenges traditional perceptions of what makes a successful cyclist. This versatility not only broadens the scope for young athletes but also encourages them to develop diverse skills rather than specializing too early in their careers. As he continues to perform across various terrains and race types, he emphasizes the importance of adaptability and continuous learning in the sport.

Pogačar actively engages with the cycling community through grassroots initiatives and youth programs. His involvement in events aimed at promoting cycling among young people Is crucial in fostering the next generation of athletes. By attending local races, clinics, and community gatherings, he connects with aspiring cyclists, providing mentorship and encouragement. This hands-on approach helps cultivate a supportive environment that inspires youth to pursue cycling as a sport and hobby, ensuring the continued growth and popularity of cycling.

Pogačar's advocacy for environmental sustainability has made a significant impact on the cycling community. He champions eco-friendly practices within the sport, urging fellow cyclists and teams to adopt more sustainable approaches to training and racing. This includes promoting the use of renewable energy, reducing waste at events, and raising awareness about the environmental challenges facing the world. His commitment to sustainability positions him as a role model for athletes, demonstrating that professional sports can align with environmental responsibility.

Pogačar's influence also extends to the global cycling culture, as he embodies a new generation of athletes who prioritize inclusivity and diversity within the sport. His approachable personality and openness to connect with fans and fellow cyclists contribute to a more welcoming atmosphere in cycling. By promoting values of sportsmanship, respect, and camaraderie, he helps build a community where individuals from diverse backgrounds feel encouraged to participate and thrive.

Pogačar's success has revitalized interest in cycling in Slovenia, inspiring a wave of enthusiasm for the sport. His achievements have not only drawn attention to local talent but have also encouraged investment in cycling infrastructure, youth programs, and competitive opportunities within the country. As a prominent figure, he has become a source of national pride, fostering a culture of cycling in Slovenia that continues to grow.

Tadej Pogačar's contributions to the sport of cycling encompass his remarkable achievements, advocacy for sustainability, and commitment to nurturing the next generation of athletes. Through his performance, engagement with the community, and promotion of inclusivity, he has made a lasting impact that extends beyond the competitive arena. Pogačar's legacy will undoubtedly influence the future of cycling, inspiring new generations to pursue their passion for the sport while promoting values of excellence, responsibility, and community.

CONCLUSION

Tadej Pogačar's journey through the world of cycling exemplifies the profound impact that a dedicated athlete can have on their sport and beyond. From his early beginnings in

Slovenia to his remarkable achievements on the international stage, Pogačar has not only redefined the standards of excellence in competitive cycling but has also inspired countless individuals to pursue their passions with fervor and commitment. His legacy is characterized by a blend of exceptional talent, hard work, and an unwavering dedication to uplifting the cycling community and promoting positive change. One of the most significant aspects of Pogačar's legacy is his ability to resonate with young cyclists and aspiring athletes. He serves as a beacon of hope and inspiration for those who dream of making their mark in the sport. His achievements demonstrate that with relentless determination and resilience, greatness is within reach. This message is particularly powerful for young cyclists who often face challenges and setbacks in their journeys. By openly sharing his experiences and engaging with the youth, Pogačar cultivates a supportive environment that encourages them to believe in their abilities and work towards their goals. His relatability and approachability make him not just a champion on the bike, but also a role model in life.

Pogačar's contributions to the cycling community extend beyond his personal success. His active involvement in youth programs and grassroots initiatives underscores his commitment to nurturing the next generation of cyclists. By encouraging young athletes to participate in cycling, he helps foster a culture of inclusivity and passion for the sport. Pogačar's hands-on approach in connecting with aspiring cyclists emphasizes the importance of mentorship and community support, paving the way for future stars in the cycling world. This dedication to youth development ensures that cycling continues to thrive and evolve, ultimately benefiting the sport as a whole.

Pogačar's influence is further amplified by his advocacy for environmental sustainability. In an era where climate change poses significant challenges, his commitment to promoting

eco-friendly practices within the cycling community

Printed in the USA
CPSIA information can be obtained
at www.ICGtesting.com
LVHW011945221124
797266LV00003B/464